Archaeology for Young Explorers

Uncovering History at Colonial Williamsburg

By

Patricia Samford

and David L. Ribblett

Patricia Samford

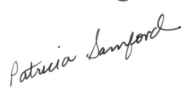

The Colonial Williamsburg Foundation
Williamsburg, Virginia

To Mary Brodnax
the young girl whose ring was found behind Shields Tavern

2020 19 18 17 16 15 14 13 12   7 8 9 10

Library of Congress Cataloging-in-Publication Data
Samford, Patricia.
    Archaeology for young explorers; uncovering history at
Colonial Williamsburg/by Patricia Samford and David L.
Ribblett.
        p.   cm.
    ISBN 0-87935-089-X
    1. Williamsburg (Va.)—Antiquities—Juvenile literature.
I. Ribblett, David L., 1958– . II. Title
F234.W7S26 1995
975.5 425202—dc20   94-40017
                                        CIP
                                        AC

The Frenchman's Map on pages 16–17 is reproduced
courtesy of Earl Gregg Swem Library, College of
William and Mary.

Thomas Jefferson's measured drawing of the
Governor's Palace on page 54 is reproduced courtesy
of the Massachusetts Historical Society.

Book design: Ken Scaglia and Helen M. Olds

Printed in China

ISBN-13: 978-0-87935-089-5

The Colonial Williamsburg Foundation
PO Box 1776
Williamsburg, Virginia 23187-1776
www.history.org

Manufactured by Everbest Printing Co. Ltd.
Guangdong, China
PO #364163 8/17/2012
Cohort: Batch 1

Contents

What Is Archaeology?

Digging to uncover information about how people lived in the past is called *archaeology*. Scientists who do this work are called *archaeologists*. They have made many important discoveries.

In 1922, after a long search, archaeologist Howard Carter found the *tomb* of King Tutankhamen, an Egyptian *pharaoh*. When he broke the seal on the door, the vault had been sealed for over three thousand years. Carter's assistant asked, "Can you see anything?" And indeed

A ceramic jug found in Williamsburg.

he could. The light of the archaeologist's lantern reflected on the "boy-king's" golden treasures. There were beds, thrones, chariots, and jewelry. "Yes, wonderful things!" Carter exclaimed. From the riches, he learned much about ancient Egypt. Howard Carter later put them on display in museums so people all over the world could learn about early Egypt.

Archaeologist Howard Carter and an assistant examine the elaborate coffin of King Tut.

One August morning almost two thousand years ago, Mount Vesuvius, a volcano near Pompeii, Italy, erupted. Over six feet of scorching volcanic ash and stone buried the entire city. Some people escaped by boat or on foot. Others stayed behind to gather their valuables or to hide in their homes. They were smothered by ashes and fumes. In 1748, archaeologists began to dig up the city of Pompeii. Deep under the thick ash they found tables still set for breakfast and people huddled in their cellars. They even found a chained guard dog who had struggled to free himself from the deadly ash.

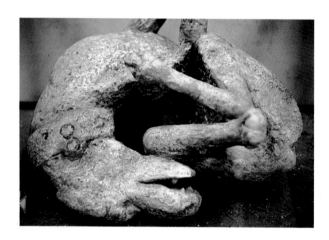

Archaeologists were able to preserve images of the victims of the Mount Vesuvius eruption by pouring plaster into the hollow spaces their bodies left behind in the ash. This guard dog is still chained at his post.

A plaster cast of a man struggling to free himself from the choking ash.

One of the thousands of life-size terra-cotta soldiers excavated from the tomb of Chinese Emperor Ch'in Shih Huang Ti.

In 1974, Chinese peasants made an incredible discovery near their village. Under the red clay soil, they found more than six thousand life-size soldiers, horses, and chariots in battle formation. They were all made of a type of pottery called terra-cotta. These lifelike warriors had been buried over two thousand years ago. People then believed that the soldiers would guard the tomb of Chinese Emperor Ch'in Shih Huang Ti. The tomb still has not been excavated. Who knows what treasures are in it?

7

Archaeologists uncovered the remains of the fort at Wolstenholme Towne.

On a peaceful morning in March 1622, another major event happened. In Wolstenholme Towne, on the James River in Virginia, a group of native American Indians sat down to breakfast with English colonists. Suddenly, the Indians grabbed the colonists' own tools and weapons and killed many of the settlers. Afterward, the Indians burned the village. They resented these English intruders. For a long time, the village of Wolstenholme Towne lay buried. In the 1970s, Colonial Williamsburg archaeologists uncovered the colonists' graves, houses, and traces of their burned fort. Then this dramatic episode in American history was rediscovered.

Archaeology has helped restore Colonial Williamsburg's buildings to their eighteenth-century appearance.

These are just a few of the amazing discoveries made by archaeologists. In this book you will learn about the archaeologists who work at Colonial Williamsburg, a town restored to the way it looked in the 1700s. By digging in places where people lived and worked two hundred years ago, they learn about the lives of early Americans.

How Do Archaeologists Know Where to Dig?

One of the questions most often asked by visitors to an archaeological *site* is "Why did you decide to dig here?" Archaeologists at Colonial Williamsburg dig where colonial Americans lived. Like a detective searches for clues to solve a mystery, archaeologists also look for clues about good places to dig, or *excavate*. Archaeologists look for two types of evidence. Have you ever lost a button or change while playing in your yard? If so, you have left *physical evidence* of your having been there. Later, you might have written in your diary or in a letter that you had lost the button or money in the yard. Then you have also left written or *documentary evidence* of your having been there.

Archaeologists have uncovered a brick foundation wall revealing where a building once stood.

Physical Evidence

People almost always leave clues, physical traces, of where they have lived. There are many types of physical evidence. Building foundations, broken pottery, animal bones, or other items that are left behind by people are all physical evidence. Archaeologists use these items, called *artifacts*, to help them find places to dig.

Sites are the places where archaeologists dig. Archaeologists dig small holes called test units where they hope to find artifacts. If artifacts are found, more digging is done on the site. Occasionally, sites are found by accident. Sometimes a farmer's plow uncovers physical evidence. When fields are plowed for planting corn or wheat, a plow often brings buried artifacts to the surface. By recording the location of these finds, archaeologists can pinpoint sites. Sometimes sites are found during the construction of new buildings or as a result of landscaping. Many times Williamsburg archaeologists are called to a site because bulldozers have uncovered some evidence of colonial life. Construction work often stops until the archaeologists explore the site further.

Pottery artifacts like these, often uncovered during construction, can help archaeologists find sites.

Documentary Evidence

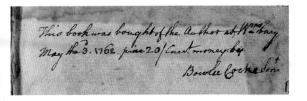

People leave records, or *documents,* of where they have been, where they have lived, and what they have done. They write diaries, letters, newspapers, and court records. A letter might describe a visit to a colonial *tavern* that stood in a now empty lot. This would be *documentary evidence* of the building's location. Archaeologists know if the lot were excavated, they would find evidence of the tavern's foundation and some artifacts. This evidence would tell them more about taverns in the colonial days. Such documents often provide clues that help archaeologists find sites.

In 1926, a unique map of Williamsburg was found at the College of William and Mary. It is called the "Frenchman's Map." It was drawn in 1781 by an unknown French soldier to help the army assign winter quarters. The map gives a bird's-eye view of Williamsburg at the end of the Revolutionary War. The plan of the town shows three main streets and cross streets. It also shows creeks and ravines, yards with fences around them, and all the buildings. The map shows buildings that are no longer standing. Colonial Williamsburg archaeologists know that they will find the building's foundations if they dig in that area. As a result, the "Frenchman's Map" has helped Williamsburg archaeologists choose where to dig.

The note at the top of this page was written in a book that had been purchased in Williamsburg.

This document is a receipt dated May 8, 1766, for William Geddy.

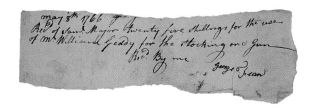

This ledger shows several subscriptions to the Virginia Gazette *newspaper.*

A letter from George Washington written in December 1782 and mailed from Newburgh, New York.

The *"Frenchman's Map,"* believed to have been drawn by a soldier in 1781, has aided archaeologists in choosing places to explore.

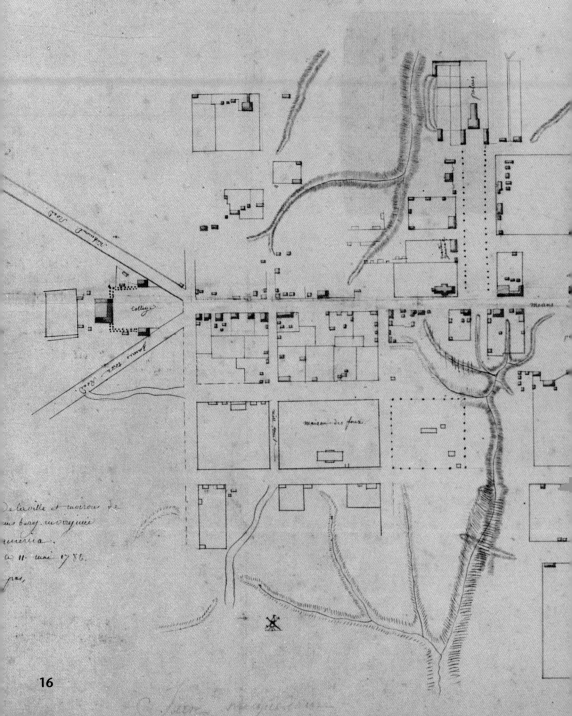

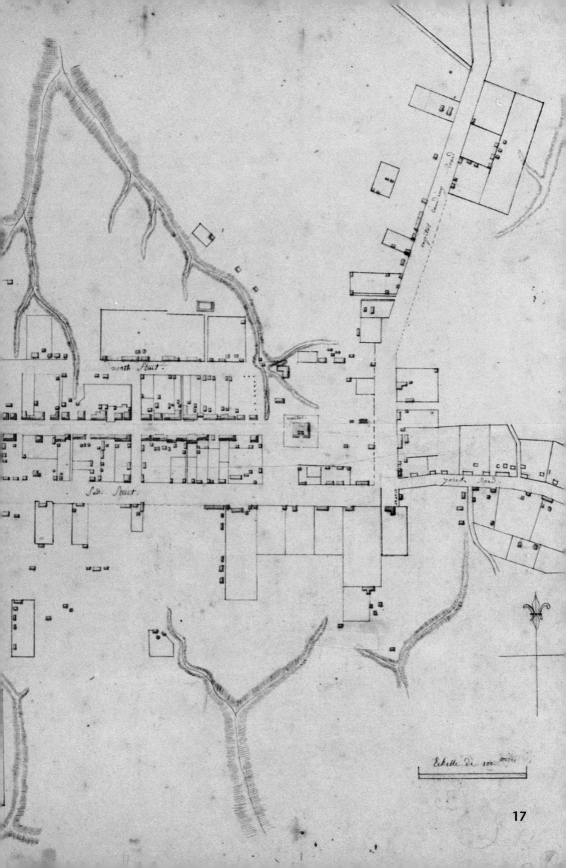

Documentary Clues for the Archaeologist

Physical and documentary evidence give archaeologists clues about where to dig. A diary is an example of documentary evidence. Here is an imaginary entry from the diary of a young boy named Jack Randolph. After reading it, make a list of all the things you might find if you were an archaeologist digging in Jack Randolph's yard.

September 7, 1779

I woke up today when I heard the rooster crowing in the chicken coop. In the morning I played marbles in the yard with my friend John. We lost two of my favorite marbles. When I went inside Mother was upset because the baby had knocked her favorite bowl off the table. It fell on the floor and broke into a hundred tiny pieces. She had to sweep the pieces out the door. Our old dog Pete died today. He was very crippled after he broke his leg last year. We buried him behind the smokehouse. We had a special dinner in honor of Father's return home from England. We ate oysters, fish, pork, chicken, and a delicious dessert. I helped Mother clean up the kitchen after dinner. I threw the leftover bones in the old abandoned well. We saved the oyster shells to cover the path to the garden. Before I went to bed, my sister Nan and I tried to catch fireflies. I went to bed early because tomorrow Father and I are going to build a new fence around the vegetable garden.

A Colonial Diary

Sally Cary Fairfax was a young girl who grew up near present-day Washington, D. C. During the years 1771 and 1772, Sally kept a diary. She recorded many events in her life. Once she visited Mount Vernon, the home of George Washington. Several entries in Sally's diaries will be helpful to archaeologists when they dig in her yard. For example, Sally wrote on January 3, 1772: "On Friday . . . came John Vain, to undertake the building of the hen house." *From this, archaeologists learn that Sally's family had a henhouse built in early 1772. The information will help archaeologists identify the henhouse after it is excavated. It also tells them when the henhouse was built.*

Do you keep a diary or journal? If you do, what have you written that could be used by archaeologists to help find sites or explain things they might find in your yard?

List what you might find in Jack Randolph's yard

How Do Artifacts End Up in the Ground?

There are many ways that artifacts end up in the ground. They can be thrown away on purpose, lost by accident, or become buried as the result of a disaster. A broken bottle is an example of something thrown away; buttons are often lost; after a fire, sometimes the foundations of a building are all that is left.

Discard

Think about what types of items you throw away in a normal day. After a breakfast of bacon and eggs, you throw away eggshells. A paper bag, sandwich wrappings, and a plastic straw are discarded after lunch at McDonald's. Chicken bones, potato peelings, and a broken dish or glass remain from dinner. In the evening, you clean your closet and throw away some broken toys and old homework. All of these things make their way into the garbage can. What would someone learn about you if they found them two hundred years from now?

At a mock site, kids are given the opportunity to experience archaeology.

There was no garbage pickup in colonial days. Instead, early Americans buried their trash in holes in their own yards. These holes were called trash pits. Trash reveals much about people. Archaeologists consider trash pits a great find. In Williamsburg trash pits, archaeologists discover broken utensils, dishes, bottles, bones, nails, and other items.

Not all colonial trash pits are located behind houses. Some are found behind the places where people worked. For example, John Brush was a gunsmith in Williamsburg. On his land archaeologists excavated gun parts and tools that Brush used to make guns. At the Anthony Hay shop, where woodworkers made furniture, pieces of tables and chairs were found. Behind an *apothecary shop*, bottles and jars used for storing medicines were discovered. These items help archaeologists learn where businesses were located and how they were run. If you were an archaeologist and found a trash pit filled with horseshoes, what conclusions could you make?

Loss

Have you ever found a marble on the playground and wondered who lost it? Some artifacts found on archaeological sites find their way into the ground after being lost. Unlike artifacts that were thrown away on purpose, lost objects are usually small and unbroken. They include things that people would not normally throw away, like coins, jewelry, buttons, and thimbles. Archaeologists do not often find coins or jewelry. People who lost valuable items generally searched for them.

Sometimes archaeologists do find valuable items that appear to have been lost. While excavating around an eighteenth-century tavern, Williamsburg archaeologists discovered a small gold ring. Written inside the ring were the words "Fear God Mary Brodnax." By studying documents, archaeologists learned that Mary Brodnax was the young daughter of a Williamsburg goldsmith. Mary probably lost the ring while playing in the tavern yard with the innkeeper's three daughters.

Disaster

Archaeological sites and their artifacts can result from a disaster. Some disasters, like an earthquake or the volcanic eruption that destroyed the city of Pompeii, can occur naturally. Although disasters are rare, they help show us how people were living when the tragedies occurred.

Another way a site can be preserved is as a result of fire. Archaeologists digging at the site of a hospital in Williamsburg found evidence of the tragic fire that destroyed the building in 1885. Because the roof collapsed into the hospital as it burned, many rooms were preserved just as they were left when people fled the fire. Crates of medicine bottles and medical supplies were uncovered in the hospital storeroom. One of the more intriguing discoveries made at the hospital was a patients' room. In this room were two iron beds. Underneath each was a *chamber pot*. Pig and chicken bones were found between the charred floorboards. The patients probably tossed the bones under the beds after dinner. At

the foot of each bed, where clothing had been hung, were clusters of glass buttons. The buttons must have dropped to the floor when the clothing caught on fire. Archaeologists carefully examined this room and others like it. They were able to learn more about hospital conditions and patient care in nineteenth-century Virginia.

By figuring out how artifacts end up buried in the ground, archaeologists can better understand the things they find.

The fire that burned for two days destroyed Eastern State Hospital but helped preserve information for archaeologists.

How Did Thomas Jefferson's Toothbrush End Up Here?

Sometimes archaeologists are not sure how a particular artifact ended up in the ground. Beside the home of Thomas Everard, a mayor of Williamsburg who lived across the street from the Governor's Palace, archaeologists found a small bone handle. They believed it was from a toothbrush or some other item from a man's shaving kit. What makes the handle very interesting is that it has the inscription "THOS JEFFERSON." on it.

Thomas Jefferson's toothbrush?

Archaeologists cannot be sure how the toothbrush ended up there. However, they have an idea. When he was the governor of Virginia from 1779 to 1780, Jefferson lived in the Governor's Palace. Maybe Jefferson left the handle behind when he moved to Richmond in 1780. The Governor's house burned to the ground in 1781. Much of the rubble that was left after the fire was dumped in the empty lot next to Thomas Everard's house. Jefferson's toothbrush must have been mixed in with the rubble.

Can you think of other ways Thomas Jefferson's toothbrush could have ended up buried in the yard across the street from his house?

Trash Can Archaeology

One of the ways archaeologists learn about the people they study is through analyzing the artifacts that are left behind. In this activity, you can study a group of artifacts in the same way that archaeologists would. On the following page is the garbage from 502 South Main Street. Carefully observe the artifacts deposited in the trash. What do they tell you about the residents of this house? Write your conclusions.

Suppose you have been examining this family's garbage bag each week for a year and it always contained an average of eight soda cans a week. Suddenly one week, the cans stop appearing in the garbage. What reasons can you think of to explain this change?

How many of the items shown would survive if they were buried in the ground for two hundred years? If you analyzed only those artifacts that still remained, would you change your conclusions about the residents of 502 South Main Street?

_____

_____

_____

_____

_____

_____

_____

_____

_____

_____

_____

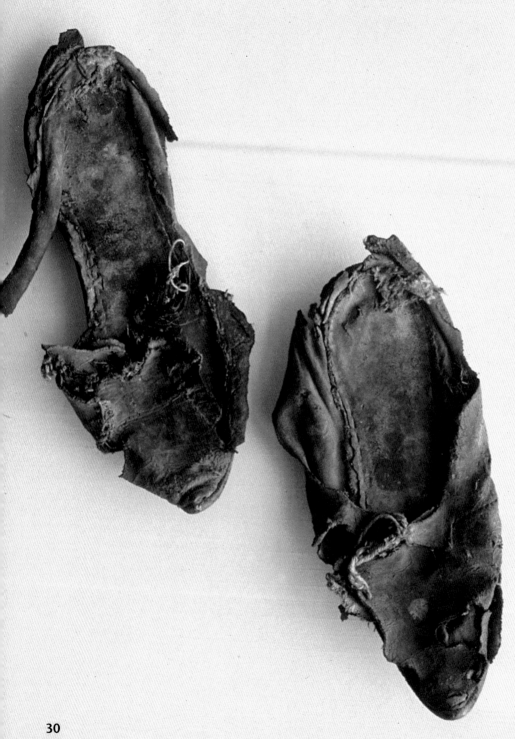

What Do Archaeologists Find?

Archaeologists look for objects associated with the culture of the people they are studying. For example, on a Pueblo Indian site in Arizona, archaeologists would look for objects connected with Southwestern Indians. If archaeologists wanted to study Aztec Indian architecture, they would travel to Mexico to excavate an Aztec city. Archaeologists at Colonial Williamsburg find many artifacts that were used every day by colonial Americans.

The remains of a typical farthing of 1769. The small change available for use in the English colonies in North America consisted mainly of standard English halfpennies.

Shoes found at the Wetherburn's Tavern site.

Lord Dunmore's gold-painted plates (above). Pipe stems and pipe bowls (left).

Pottery

Many different types of artifacts are made of pottery. Pottery is molded clay that is baked in a very hot oven called a *kiln*. Pottery objects can be plain like a kitchen mixing bowl. They also can be very decorative, like Lord Dunmore's gold-painted plates found at the Governor's Palace. Most pottery objects were used for preparing and eating food. Pottery can tell archaeologists many things. Learning where the pottery was made tells them what countries the colonists were doing business with. Studying the decoration and shape of pottery can help archaeologists date a site.

Not all pottery objects were used in the kitchen. Wig curlers, tobacco pipes, and flowerpots were also made of pottery.

Glass

Most of the artifacts found at Williamsburg are wine bottle glass fragments. Wine bottles were expensive in the 1700s, so colonial Americans handled them carefully and reused them for a number of purposes. Williamsburg archaeologists have also excavated unbroken wine bottles that had contained milk, lead shot, traces of tar, or cherry pits. Archaeologists digging at Wetherburn's Tavern found thirty-five unbroken wine bottles that were filled with cherries. Around the year 1750, someone buried these bottles of cherries outside the kitchen wall for an unknown reason and then forgot them.

Drinking glasses, medicine bottles, glass beads, and window panes are also uncovered in Williamsburg. But the most unusual glass artifact found in the restored town was an artificial human eye!

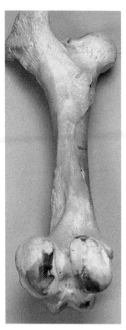

Food Remains

Many artifacts found on Williamsburg sites are the remains of colonial meals. The bones of chickens, pigs, cows, and wild animals are found in the eighteenth-century city. From these remains, archaeologists can tell what meats the colonists were eating and how they were cooked. Archaeologists also find many fish bones, oyster shells, and crab claws because Williamsburg is near several rivers and creeks. Fresh seafood was an important part of the colonial person's diet.

Archaeologists also study seeds and pollen found on sites. This helps them learn what vegetables, fruits, grains, and spices people ate. Seeds from fruits and vegetables are often very small. Archaeologists sift the soil carefully through a window screen to find them. Pollen grains can survive hundreds of years in the soil. They cannot be seen without a microscope.

Metal Objects

Metal objects can be made of iron, copper, brass, pewter, silver, or gold. Objects that needed to be strong for daily use were made of iron. These included shovels, garden hoes, nails, door locks, keys, scissors, cooking pots, and horseshoes. Decorative buttons, buckles, candlesticks, and thimbles were usually made of copper because it could be polished to a shiny finish. In an eighteenth-century vegetable garden at the Shields Tavern site, excavators discovered a round sleigh bell made of brass. Archaeologists believe the bell may have been hung in the garden to scare away hungry birds. Objects made from very expensive metals like gold and silver are rarely found.

Children's Artifacts

Archaeologists do not find toys on every site that they dig in Williamsburg. However, they have discovered a variety of artifacts that belonged to children. Clay and glass marbles, arms and legs from china dolls, pottery tea sets, bone dominoes, musical instruments called Jew's harps, and miniature cast-iron cannons are some of the toys they have found.

Features

Some of the things that archaeologists find are called features, not artifacts. Features include foundation walls, brick and shell walkways, fence posts, wells, and graves. Archaeologists carefully map and record the locations of features to help them reconstruct a site. When the information from features and from artifacts is combined, archaeologists have a clearer picture of life in eighteenth-century Virginia.

It is important to draw carefully the features that have been found.

Physical Clues for the Archaeologist

Archaeologists study physical evidence, called artifacts, of the past. Artifacts are objects that people used in their everyday lives. The pot you cook in and the dishes you eat from are artifacts. The chairs and tables in your dining room and the lamp and dresser in your bedroom are artifacts. Your toothbrush is an artifact. So are the chicken bones you threw away after supper last night. Artifacts are everywhere. Artifacts include toys, clothing, tools, furniture, gadgets, and weapons. Even the buildings where you live and go to school are artifacts. Look around you. You are surrounded by artifacts.

Is the tree outside your window an artifact? No, not unless you cut it down and use it for something. If you hollow it out to make a canoe or remove a branch and whittle a whistle, you have created an artifact. If you boil the roots for tea or burn the wood for heat, you have made something from the tree.

List below all of the items on top of your bedroom dresser or bedside table. If archaeologists found these items two hundred years from now, what could they learn about you?

_____   _____
_____   _____
_____   _____
_____   _____
_____   _____
_____   _____

GEDDY HOUSE
1980
OVERVIEW
OF N TEST UNIT
122N/221E
7/26/04
CB
1:20

LIMIT OF EXCAVATION

122N
221E

LIMIT OF EXCAVATION

?

CONCENTRATION
OF
BRICK RUBBLE

WALKWAY
BASE

OCT. '44

OCT. '45

How Do Archaeologists Dig?

Archaeology often appears to visitors to be a slow, dull process. An archaeological site can only be excavated one time. Therefore, archaeologists must work slowly and carefully. Digging a site is like reading a book in which pages disappear after they are read. It is not possible to turn back and reread pages for any missed or forgotten information. Archaeologists destroy a site as it is dug. It can only be "read" once, like the disappearing book. Archaeologists must follow certain methods in order to excavate and record a site properly.

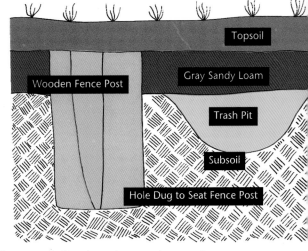

The ground beneath your feet is like a layer cake. Over time, the soil builds up into layers of various colors and textures. Each layer represents a different period of time. Archaeologists remove each layer of soil, one at a time, beginning at the top, or ground surface, and digging down. As a rule, the deeper they dig, the farther back in time they go. Archaeologists stop digging when they reach the undisturbed layers, called *subsoil*. Subsoil was formed before man lived on the site. Eight to twelve inches of soil builds up every one hundred years. So, in Williamsburg, archaeologists usually have to dig down two feet to reach things thrown away in the 1700s.

The tools that archaeologists use to dig and record their sites are ones that you probably have in your own home or garage.

Trowel — a hand tool used to scrape away soil layers.

Bucket — a pail used to hold and carry soil.

Dustpan — used for removing excavated soil.

Paintbrush — brush with soft bristles used to clean soil away from fragile artifacts.

Graph Paper — paper with horizontal and vertical lines used to map a site.

Ruler — used for measuring and drawing site maps accurately.

Camera — used to make a photographic record of the site as digging progresses.

Computer — used for storing and analyzing information uncovered on archaeological sites.

Using trowels, archaeologists begin slowly to scrape away layers of soil in small amounts. They always keep careful watch for artifacts. Once an artifact is found, it is carefully removed from the ground and placed into a bag. A description of where the artifact was found is written on the bag. The loosened soil is dumped into a bucket and carried to a sifting area. Then the soil is poured into a sifter made of wire mesh screen. When the sifter is shaken, the soil falls through. Any artifacts that were missed in the scraping process are left in the sifter. As archaeologists remove soil layers, they keep careful records of the artifacts they

Helpers carefully sift soil to make sure no artifacts have been missed.

An artifact is identified and numbered as soon as it is removed from the soil.

find, where the objects were found, and what the soil looked like. Later, these notes will help them decide what happened at the site in the past.

When artifacts such as bones, iron, or wood remain buried in the ground for hundreds of years, they become fragile. Archaeologists must be very careful when removing them. If the artifacts are damaged, valuable information may be lost. Special tools and methods are needed so that these objects can be lifted from the ground without harm. Archaeologists excavating Wolstenholme Towne near Williamsburg found many artifacts. They found skeletons, weapons, and even armor that the colonists had brought from England.

One of the most fascinating artifacts was a seventeenth-century helmet. The steel helmet had been buried for so long that it felt like wet cardboard. Archaeologists were afraid the softened helmet might collapse if they removed it from the soil. They changed their usual method of excavation to protect the helmet. Instead of removing the helmet from the soil at the site, they cut out the soil around the helmet and took the big block of soil back to the lab. There they

The excavation of a well at Wolstenholme Towne uncovered this seventeenth-century helmet.

made the helmet stronger with plastic mesh before it was excavated. This excavation and restoration process took months. All of the hard work was worth it, though, because the archaeologists had discovered the first such helmet ever found in America.

Now you know why archaeologists work so slowly when they are digging a site!

The helmet after conservation treatment in the laboratory. It was the first helmet of its kind found in America.

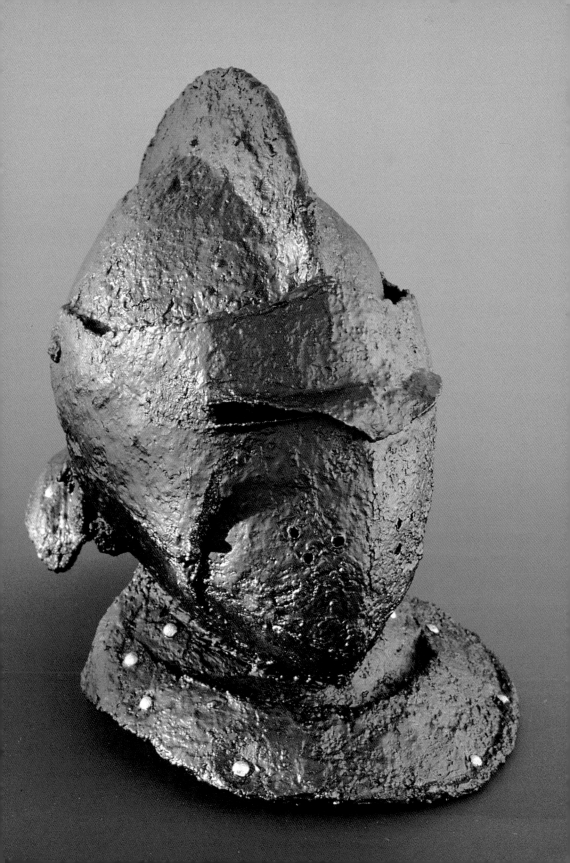

Archaeology Anagram

```
A  R  T  I  F  A  C  T  S  Q  A  Z  S  G
V  R  F  E  D  C  X  R  E  C  O  R  D  R
B  U  C  K  E  T  H  O  B  N  Y  U  J  A
E  Z  A  H  Q  O  P  W  L  I  K  S  M  P
X  W  S  C  A  D  R  E  F  B  R  U  S  H
C  J  N  H  C  E  Y  L  T  R  G  B  B  V
A  R  C  H  A  E  O  L  O  G  I  S  T  S
V  M  U  L  R  I  P  L  Q  O  W  O  R  I
A  S  B  J  E  D  K  C  O  L  Y  I  T  F
T  C  X  L  F  K  R  A  V  G  B  L  N  T
E  K  P  N  U  M  O  M  C  H  Y  F  Q  E
Q  A  Z  X  L  A  Y  E  R  S  W  E  D  R
Z  X  C  O  V  B  I  R  A  D  S  F  U  Q
Q  W  D  U  S  T  P  A  N  E  R  T  Y  P
```

Words

ARCHAEOLOGISTS
ARCHAEOLOGY
ARTIFACTS
BRUSH
BUCKET
CAMERA
CAREFUL

DUSTPAN
EXCAVATE
GRAPH
LAYERS
RECORD
SIFTER
SUBSOIL
TROWEL

What Do Archaeologists Do with What They Find?

Archaeologists excavated behind the Williamsburg home of Peyton Randolph, the president of the first Continental Congress. They found several pieces of pottery, fragments of light green glass, an iron key, and a pig's jawbone. The artifacts were placed in a plastic bag. On the bag, they labeled where the artifacts had been found. At the end of the day the bag was taken to the lab. The artifact processing takes place in the lab. The artifacts are washed, numbered, mended, and conserved. Then they can be studied in detail.

Washing

First, the artifacts are placed on a tray made of screen and carefully washed. A toothbrush is used to scrub them under running water. The trays are then placed on a rack and left to dry overnight.

Numbering

Each artifact is given a number showing where it was found. Using permanent ink, an archaeologist writes a small number on each pottery, bone, and glass artifact. A coating of nail polish protects the number. Next, a complete list is made of all the artifacts that were found at the Peyton Randolph site.

Mending

The fragments of pottery and glass are put back together. This is much like doing a jigsaw puzzle. After fitting the pieces together, an archaeologist glues them into place. Then the artifact is set into a box of sand for support while the glue hardens. Archaeologists study the reconstructed fragments found in the yard of the Peyton Randolph House. They see that they have found a teacup and a medicine bottle.

Conservation

Sometimes objects like the steel helmet from Wolstenholme Towne need special attention. The key and the jawbone from the Peyton Randolph site will eventually disintegrate unless they are treated. The process of cleaning and preserving these items is known as *conservation*. Some objects are easier to preserve than others. For example, the pig's jawbone only requires soaking in a special chemical that will keep the bone from falling apart. The iron key, however, needs a longer process of treatment for its preservation. In the ground for two hundred years, the iron key became completely covered with rust. Archaeologists remove the rust from iron objects by using a machine that works like a miniature sandblaster, blowing out a powder at high pressure. After the rust is removed, the key must be soaked in purified water to remove any salts that would cause it to rust again. Even with the water being changed daily, the soaking process can take up to a year. Afterward, the artifact is oven-dried overnight and coated with a protective wax.

Most people think that excavation is a slow process. However, lab work and examining the artifacts take even longer. For every day of digging on the site, three days are needed for studying in the lab!

*Archaeologists excavate the skeletons
of a man and woman who were killed at
Wolstenholme Towne in 1622.*

Bones, Bones, Bones

How do archaeologists identify the bones that they find? At Colonial Williamsburg, bones are identified by a specialist called a zooarchaeologist. *A zoologist is a scientist who studies animals, and so a zooarchaeologist is someone who examines animal bones found on archaeological sites. Just as you can look at an animal and identify whether it is a chicken, cow, or pig, a zooarchaeologist can look at only a bone and tell the same thing. Zooarchaeologists learn how to identify bones by studying many different kinds of animal skeletons.*

What can archaeologists learn by studying a human skeleton? Archaeologists uncovered 158 skeletons in the Governor's Palace garden. They were able to learn much about the people who were buried there. Measuring a skeleton from head to toe gives a person's height. Teeth, and the development of leg and arm bones, are clues to a person's age at death. Teeth can also tell archaeologists the person's race. The shape of a hipbone indicates whether a skeleton was a man or woman. A person's health can also be determined. Some diseases leave scars on the bones. Broken arms or legs can be seen. Sometimes how a person died can also be discovered. For example, some of the skeletons from the Palace cemetery had cannonball or sword fragments in their bones.

Putting the Pieces Together

Artifacts are often found broken into many pieces. The broken pieces are carefully placed in a bag and taken to the lab. After the pieces are put back together, archaeologists can learn more about how people lived and used things.

Directions:

1. Photocopy the fragments or trace them along the black lines onto another sheet of paper. Cut out the fragments.

2. Lay the cut out fragments on another piece of paper.

3. Fit the fragments together. Paste or tape them on the paper.

4. Draw in what you think the missing piece may have looked like.

5. Color the mended artifact if you wish.

6. How do you think this artifact was used?

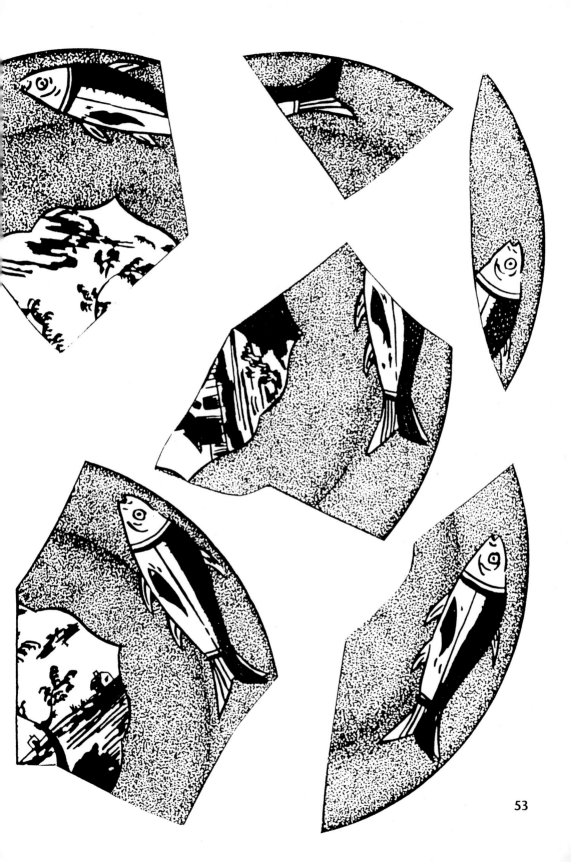

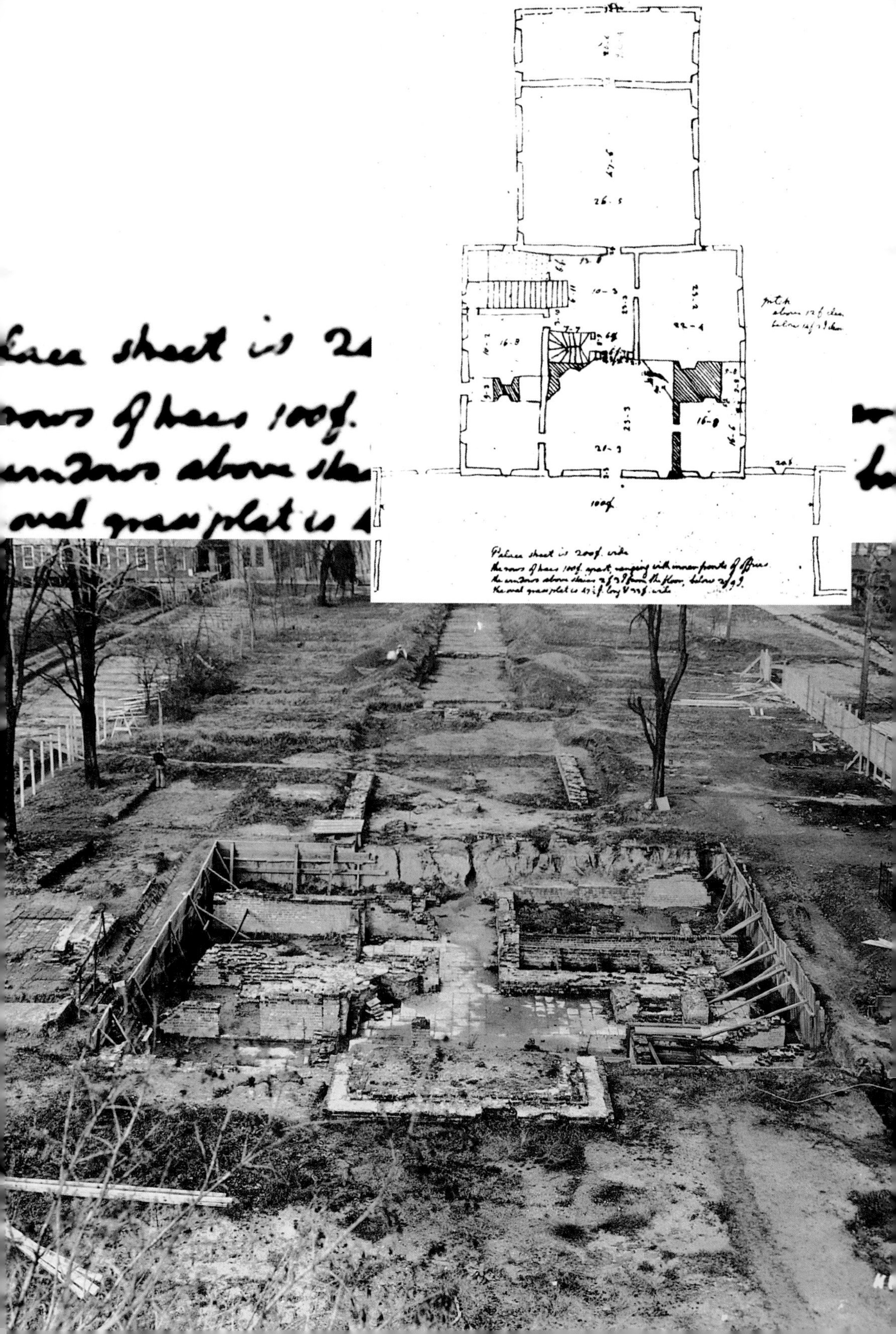

26.5
100f.
Palace street is 200f. wide

What Do Archaeologists Learn from Their Discoveries?

Archaeologists carefully examine artifacts. They also study building foundations and soil stains. Fitting all the clues together with documentary sources is like solving a puzzle. When completed, it tells about the lives of the people who lived and worked at the site. An example of this process is the site of the Governor's Palace in Colonial Williamsburg's Historic

Area. It helps us understand the life of the 1700s. The Governor's Palace was finished in 1722. It was described as the grandest house in the colony. Here the royal governor entertained his guests and managed the Virginia colony. It was the governor's home until the capital moved to Richmond in 1780. At the end of the Revolutionary War, it was used as a military hospital. Fire destroyed the Palace in 1781. The kitchen, stables, offices, and other buildings soon fell into disrepair and were torn down.

The floor plan drawn by Thomas Jefferson and the excavation of the Governor's Palace in 1930 helped in the reconstruction of the building.

In the 1920s Williamsburg's restoration began. The Governor's Palace was an important part of the reconstruction. A number of documentary sources referring to the structure were found. The Frenchman's Map showed the location of the building. An engraving showed the Palace's outside. An interior floor plan drawn by Thomas Jefferson showed the location of rooms, staircases, doorways, and windows. In spite of these documentary sources, a number of important questions remained. They had to be answered before the building could be reconstructed. What did the Palace look like inside? How was the Palace furnished? What other buildings were on the Palace property? Archaeologists came to the rescue. Only by excavating the site could these questions be answered.

In 1930, archaeologists began to uncover the foundations of the once elegant mansion. They removed three collapsed stories of burnt brick. The archaeologists discovered that the Palace's cellars were not damaged. The artifacts told what the inside of the building looked like at the time of the fire. Archaeologists found pieces of black and white marble tile from the floor in the entrance hall. Fragments of walnut

paneling from the walls were excavated. A marble mantelpiece that once decorated the fireplace in the parlor was also discovered. It has carvings of deer beneath a tree.

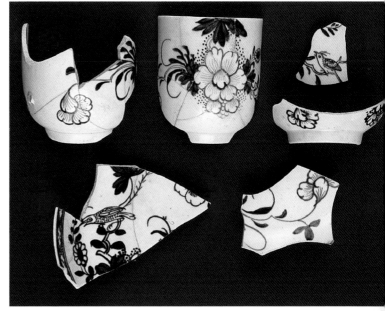

Artifacts were found inside the cellar and around the Palace yard. They were evidence of the house's furnishings. Archaeologists found fashionable wineglasses and fancy dinner plates. These showed that the governor was used to a grand lifestyle. Researchers used these artifacts and a list of Palace furnishings written in 1770 to refurnish the mansion.

Several buildings around the Palace were uncovered by the archaeologists. There was a laundry building where clothes and sheets were washed. The laundry was identified by its system of wells and drains. Archaeologists discovered that the governor's food was kept cold in an egg-shaped icehouse that was twenty-five feet deep.

Pottery and glass excavated from the site have made it possible to redecorate the rooms of the Governor's Palace.

In colonial days, various governors wrote about the elaborate gardens around the Palace. When archaeologists excavated the Palace grounds, they discovered traces of large flower beds. A fish pond, walkways, garden walls, and decorative flowerpots all proved that the governor's gardens were indeed beautiful. One of the most interesting finds in the garden did not tell about the governor, but rather about the house's later history. Skeletons of 156 soldiers and two nurses were evidence that the structure later served as a military hospital.

All of this information was used to reconstruct the Palace's former splendor. Visitors today can once again see the governor's residence. It has been reconstructed, furnished, and decorated based on the combination of the documentary evidence and the archaeologists' discoveries. Over four hundred buildings in Williamsburg have been restored using a similar process.

What's in a Layer?

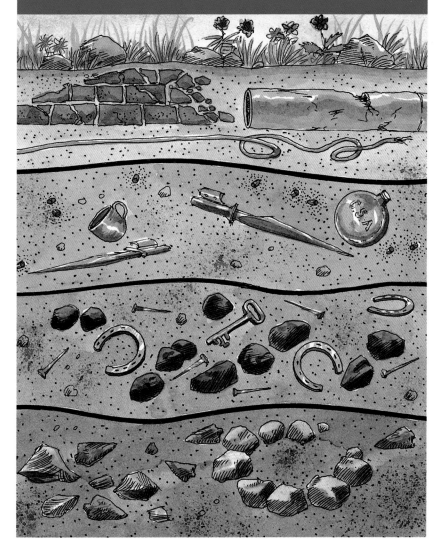

1901–2000 layer
brick foundations
water pipe
electricity cable

1801–1900 layer
bullets
bayonets
tin cup
canteen

1701–1800 layer
iron key
horseshoes
nails
charcoal

1600–1700 layer
arrowheads
chipped stones
rocks arranged in a circle

Layers of soil build up over time. People who lived within the time a layer was formed leave evidence of their lives in that layer.

Study the layers.

What do you think the property was being used for while each layer was formed? What makes you think so?

Why Is Archaeology Important at Colonial Williamsburg?

Archaeology is a method of discovering information about the past that cannot be learned in any other way. There are many reasons why archaeology is important at the Colonial Williamsburg Foundation. Many of Williamsburg's buildings could not have been rebuilt accurately without archaeology. It helps locate buildings. It also gives clues about what buildings looked like, how they were furnished, and how they were used.

When you and your family visit Colonial Williamsburg's Historic Area, many of the things you see and learn about have been influenced by the findings of archaeology. When you eat at a colonial tavern, the dishes are authentic reproductions of ones found by Williamsburg's archaeologists. Sparrows again make nests in pottery bird "bottles" just like those made in the 1700s. You walk on crushed oyster shell or brick walkways where colonial Americans once strolled. Shoes, buttons, buckles, and fabric found on Williamsburg sites are all reproduced for clothing that *interpreters* wear today.

Excavations at colonial sites were important in reconstructing and equipping the historic trades shops.

A reconstructed slave house at Great Hopes Plantation.

Archaeology also helps us learn about people who are not often mentioned in the written records. A good example is eighteenth-century African-American slaves. They had very little written about them. Slave houses were usually built of poor materials and have rarely survived. Archaeologists have dug on the sites where slave quarters once stood and have been able to learn what slave houses looked like. They know that the houses of African-Americans in Virginia were usually made of wood. The houses were built directly on the ground or around wooden posts buried in the soil. A family of four or more lived in one room. Space was restricted. Dirt floors were common in these small houses. The few household goods were often stored in holes, or cellars, dug into the cabin floor. Artifacts dug from these holes and nearby trash pits tell archaeologists what the slaves ate. The masters gave the slaves some food, and they were allowed to hunt and fish. Other items tell

Artifacts left behind by slaves provide new information on the daily life of early African-Americans.

archaeologists how slaves lived. This information is rarely found in written records.

Archaeology can also tell us how people worked in the 1700s. Documents show that James Anderson was a blacksmith in Williamsburg in the 1770s. During the Revolutionary War, one of Anderson's jobs was to provide soldiers with weapons and wagons. However, archaeology provided the details about Anderson's shop from day to day. Archaeologists mapped in the locations of artifacts on the shop floor. They were able to tell when, what, and how iron objects were being made. Pieces of window glass show where windows were located in the shop. Large numbers of nails and carriage parts in certain rooms provide information on what was being made where. Only through careful excavation could this information have been discovered.

Saving Archaeological Sites

Every day archaeological sites are being destroyed. Once a site has been destroyed, its information is lost forever. New buildings, roads, and other developments have caused the complete destruction of many archaeological sites. What if a tourist resort had been constructed on the site of Pompeii? Suppose condominiums had been built at Wolstenholme Towne? History would have never learned about these early settlements and what happened to them.

Sites have also been destroyed by people who are only interested in removing the artifacts but not in what they tell about the past. Most things archaeologists find are broken and not worth any money. But the

information for archaeologists is priceless. If grave robbers had stripped King Tut's tomb of all its treasures, we would know less today about ancient Egypt. Fortunately, laws protect many archaeological sites from development and looting. Laws also help preserve their information for the future. Not all sites are protected, however. It is our responsibility to see that they are excavated by trained archaeologists or preserved for future generations.

Glossary

Apothecary shop. An early American drugstore.

Archaeologist. A scientist who uncovers and studies the buried remains of the past.

Archaeology. The process of digging to uncover information on how people lived.

Artifact. Any object made or used by humans.

Chamber pot. A pottery bowl used as a toilet before indoor plumbing was invented.

Conservation. Specialized cleaning and treatment given to artifacts to ensure their survival.

Culture. A people's unique behaviors, beliefs, and artifacts.

Documents. Written sources, such as letters, newspapers, or maps, used to furnish information.

Excavate. To dig an archaeological site.

Interpreter. A person who explains early American life to visitors.

Kiln. A special type of oven used to bake clay at a high temperature.

Pharaoh. An Egyptian king.

Site. A location that contains evidence of human activity.

Subsoil. An undisturbed layer of soil containing nothing made or used by humans.

Tavern. A place, much like a modern hotel, where early Americans could eat or spend the night.

Tomb. A grave or an aboveground place of burial.

Zooarchaeologist. An archaeologist who studies the animal bones found on archaeological sites.